I0487162

Selling Cable:

The Direct Sales Guide for Video, Voice & Data

Selling Cable:

The Direct Sales Guide for Video, Voice & Data

By Clint Symons

Symons, Clint

ISBN -   144048466X   - paperback

This book is dedicated to the hard working people who pride themselves each day on providing video, voice and data solutions to homes across the world.

Special thanks to Shawn Broach, Michael Ortiz and Lionel Lomas for providing their experiences in cable sales.

Brief History of Cable TV

Cable television was formed in Pennsylvania during 1948. Prior to being called "cable television", the method was known as Community Antenna Television or CATV. CATV was started by John and Margaret Walson in the spring of 1948. The Walson's formed the CATV to enhance poor reception of over-the-air television signals in mountainous and remote areas. Antennas were erected on mountain tops or other high points, and homes were connected to the towers to receive the broadcast signals.

By the early 50's there were 70 cable systems nationwide serving more than 14,000 paid subscribers. Later that decade cable companies began to change focus to providing new programming choices. Within ten years there were almost 800 cable systems serving 850,000 subscribers.

In 1972 Charles Dolan and Gerald Levin of Sterling Manhattan Cable launched HBO (Home Box Office), which was the first pay-tv network. This type of programming led to the use of a national satellite distribution system.

Satellites changed the business and broadcast reach dramatically so by the end of the 80's nearly 53 million households were cable subscribers.

By the end of the 90's almost 7 of every 10 households subscribed to cable television. As cable grew in popularity, so did the companies providing the service. Larger cable companies, referred to as MSO's (Multiple System Operators), had established franchises in multiple locations.

The new millennium offered unique opportunities with technology advancements. Cable companies increased efforts to enhance their network infrastructure by investing $65 billion to build higher capacity hybrid networks of fiber optic and coaxial cable. These "broadband" networks could provide multichannel video, two-way voice, high-speed Internet access, and high definition and advanced digital video services all from a single wire to the home.

Today cable operators with two-way plant have expanded growth in "broadband" data. Cable has become the technology of choice, rivaling DSL (digital subscriber line) service, offered by phone companies.

With digital television advancements cable offers deployment of High-Definition Television (HDTV), Video-on-Demand (VOD), digital cable, and other advanced services. Competitive digital phone service gained momentum as cable introduced Voice over Internet Protocol (VoIP) telephone services.

The industry continues to thrive with cable companies focusing on providing customers video, voice and data solutions.

Top 25 Cable Providers by Subscriber Totals

	MSO	Subscribers
1	*Comcast Communications*	*24,553,000*
2	*Time Warner Cable*	*13,297,000*
3	*Cox Communications(e)*	*5,403,740*
4	*Charter Communications*	*5,162,000*
5	*Cablevision Systems*	*3,132,000*
6	*Bright House Networks LLC(e)*	*2,338,103*
7	*Mediacom LLC*	*1.321,000*
8	*Suddenlink Communications(s)*	*1,300,000*
9	*CableOne*	*701,834*
10	*Insight Communications*	*692,800*
11	*RCN Corp.*	*363,000*
12	*WideOpenWest Networks(e)*	*361,241*
13	*Bresnan Communications(e)*	*299,803*
14	*Service Electric(e)*	*288,624*
15	*Atlantic Broadband*	*285,471*
16	*Armstrong Group of Co.*	*236,187*
17	*Knology Holdings*	*230,086*
18	*Midcontinent Communications*	*201,947*
19	*Blue Ridge Communications(e)*	*179,772*
20	*Broadstripe(e)*	*157,244*
21	*General Communication*	*148,011*
22	*Buckeye CableSystem(e)*	*146,726*
23	*MetroCast Cablevision(e)*	*143,608*
24	*WaveDivision Holdings*	*141,912*
25	*MidOcean Partners (e)*	*138,810*

Source: National Cable & Telecommunications Association as of July 2008
(e)= Estimate
(s)= Source: Operator

Introduction to Direct Sales

The practice of direct sales has been around for thousands of years. People-to-people selling is a process that offers compensation for goods or services. Direct sales people have been referred to as face-to-face sellers, door-to-door or D2D sales people. They've been effective positions for sales people and the companies they represent by introducing their product and services to the consumer. Traditionally products such as books, cleaning supplies, house wares and even cosmetics have been pitched to those in the convenience of their own home.

Today direct sales still exists, providing consumers with a variety of different products and services. Companies like Stanley Steamer® and Schwan's Home Service® are just a few who have benefitted over the years from the direct sales approach. The concept of impulse buying has sparked interest again for cable providers who have jumpstarted their direct sales efforts over the last couple years

An Old Practice with a New Purpose
Even though cable providers produce more sales through conventional marketing efforts such as radio, television and direct mailings, there has been a new surge in direct selling. What cable providers have found is well trained and motivated direct sales people can combat competition by converting satellite customers to cable customers. By

placing bounties on Dish Network™ and Direct TV® customers, the cable industry has seen an incredible amount of new customer growth over the last couple years. They've even transitioned these efforts into their traditional marketing tactics with "Dump the Dish" oriented campaigns.

In the past market share has been divided by cable providers and satellite providers for consumer choices for video. Today in many markets customers have another option to choose from in fiber. With companies like AT&T® offering U-verse, and Verizon FiOS making up approximately 4% of video customers, it's crucial for cable providers to expand their sales efforts. Because of this there has been an increase in demand for direct sales positions within the cable industry nationwide.

The prime responsibility for a direct sales representative in the cable industry is sell video, voice and data products. This is accomplished by canvassing a specified area and knocking on doors of households to engage residents and sell them cable services. Each day thousands of sales people travel door to door in communities representing cable providers. Many of the top ten cable companies use direct sales people to sell their services including Comcast®, Time Warner Cable™, Cox®, Charter Cable®, Mediacom® and Insight.

Benefits of direct selling include freedom to manage time and work representing a professional company that provides value added services through cutting-edge technology. Earning potential in these positions can also be favorable. Successful representatives can make more than $150,000 each year.

Of course there are challenges faced by these sales people each day including weather, competition, long hours and sales rejection.

To be successful in direct sales an individual must possess many attributes including:

Positive Attitude

- *Possess an outgoing personality*
- *Overcome objection and handle rejection*
- *Be friendly, courteous and helpful*

Organizational Skills

- *Track and manage leads effectively*
- *Efficient with time management*
- *Strong planning and preparation*

Work Ethic

- *The drive to succeed*
- *Relentless pursuit to improve*
- *Continuous learning and development*

Building Product Knowledge
Understanding What You're Selling

Understanding product knowledge is crucial for any direct sales representative. Each direct sales rep must first understand what they are trying to sell and have product knowledge of the items offered. A direct sales rep must know what things do (the features) and how things work, and why is it of value (the benefits).

It is important that a direct sales rep express to prospective customers why they would subscribe to the cable services. What benefits will it provide to the subscriber? How will it improve their lives? Will the service save them time and money, and if so how much?

Understanding product knowledge builds confidence within each sales person so they may provide answers on the fly to consumer questions. By building product knowledge a direct sales representative gains selling confidence.

The best way to build product knowledge is by understanding the what, where, when, how and why of the cable products and services offered.

Video (Cable Video)

✓ Basic Programming

✓ Premiums & HDTV

✓ VOD (Video on Demand)

✓ Digital Video Equipment

Providing video has been the staple since the cable industry inception. As its core product, video services continue to be a prime focus for MSO's seeking to gain market share over competitors. By expanding programming, high definition channels and enhanced technologies, such as VOD, cable providers continue to grow their video offerings.

Basic Programming

Basic cable is the primary level of service offered for subscription. This programming may include retransmitted broadcast signals as well as local, regional and national cable network and public access programming.

Public Access Channels are channels set aside by a cable operator for use by the public, educational institutions, local governments, and commercial interests unaffiliated with the operator.

Basic service offerings at the system level may be offered in multiple tiers. Cable providers offer tiers that include additional national channels such as The Discovery Channel®, USA Network, TNT, A&E, The Weather Channel®, MTV, VH-1 and more. These tiers are structured to provide additional programming for higher rates of subscription.

Premium Channels

Premium channels are often referred to as pay channels or pay-tv. They represent programming that a consumer must pay additional money to subscribe and are not part of a basic cable package unless bundled in a promotion.

The demand for these premium channels can be high because of the programming offered. Over the last few years many original programs have been created and produced exclusively for these premium channels which require subscription access to view. Shows such as The Sopranos, Dexter and Weeds have all originated exclusively on premium channels.

In addition to premium channels there is also pay–per-view, often called PPV, channels. This is a type of pay-tv where viewers are charged each time they watch a special event or movie being broadcast.

HDTV Channels

High Definition Television (HDTV) provides service to digital televisions which offers twice the resolution, wider screens, higher sound and color than the standard format. With the addition of this technology the demand from viewers of HD programming has increased. Cable providers can offer select HD channels within their digital programming packages. The amount of HD programming is often determined by the amount of the digital cable package a subscriber selects. Some providers have even provided HD only tiers where subscribers only receive HD programs through their cable service.

Often network programs will carry an "HD" caption within their logo to identify the availability. There are over one hundred channels that offer HDTV within their programming including local, regional and national networks.

VOD (Video on Demand)

Video on demand provides viewers a unique way to watch films and television programs through their digital receivers. Depending on the cable provider, the service can provide access to a wide collection of material and allow the viewer to rewind, pause and fast forward the program, just like a DVD.

Video on demand originated as a pay-per-view system. Now, Video on Demand is offered by most major cable and network systems and often provides free access to thousands of previously shown television programs and movies as part of tiered packages. Video on demand does still charge fees for specific broadcasts which usually include the latest film releases.

Video on demand works in two fashions. The programs may either be streamed or downloaded to the digital receiver. The streaming system enables viewers to watch the program as it is being downloaded. The downloaded option stores the program within the digital receiver for later viewing.

A direct sales representative should know what type of technology is offered when using Video on Demand. It is also important to understand what limitations if any are placed on the footprint of the cable provider. Even though a provider may offer Video on Demand, the service may not be available to all markets served.

Digital Video Equipment

Each MSO uses different brands and models of products. A direct sales rep should obtain documentation on features and compatibility of products their cable company offers including digital receivers, digital video recording units and modems. The following products will provide a basic understanding of features offered to customers.

Digital TV Receiver

The use of a digital receiver provides cable companies a way to broadcast digital cable. These receivers act as a delivery system feeding power from the cable provider to a subscriber's television.

DCT6200 Analog/Digital, HDTV Set-top

The Motorola DCT6200 delivers high definition programming and interactive digital cable. It supports applications, graphics and typical digital TV functionality: including the interactive program guide (IPG), video on demand (VOD), and commercial-free music.

Key Features

- MPEG-2 digital video processor
- Integrated high definition
- DVI and dual 1394 (DTV) digital connectors
- Built-in MPEG analog encoder
- Two 54-860MHz Tuners
- 800 MIPS, RISC-based microprocessor
- 32 bit, 2-D / 3-D graphics
- Analog/digital video scaling (Picture in Graphics)

(Example shown)

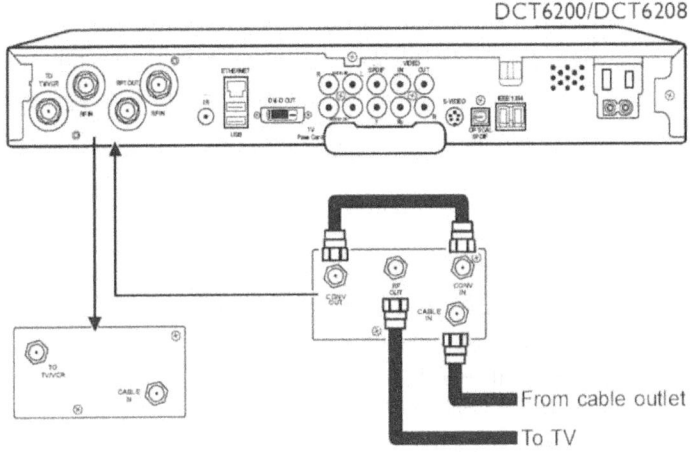

DCT6200/DCT6208

From cable outlet

To TV

Source: Motorola, Inc. (www.motorola.com)

Digital Video Recorder (DVR)

The use of a digital video recorder provides cable companies a way to broadcast digital cable. The recorder acts as a delivery system feeding power from the cable provider to a subscriber's television and allows digital recording of programs.

DCT6400 Analog/Digital, HDTV, DVR Series

This DVR set-top series combines the features of digital cable such as: programming options, interactive program guides (IPG), video on demand (VOD), and commercial-free, CD quality music — with dual-tuner, digital video recording (DVR) for watch and record capability as well as high definition television (HDTV).

Key Features

- Decodes high definition video
- Outputs HDTV in multiple video modes
- Provides dual tuner DVR functionality to pause and time shift live video
- Includes a built in DOCSIS cable modem for IP services

(Example shown)

DCT6400 Phase III

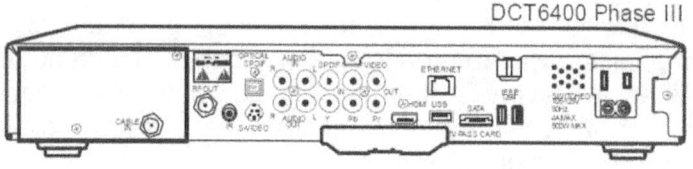

Source: Motorola, Inc. (www.motorola.com)

Interactive Program Guide

An interactive program guide (IPG), or electronic program guide (EPG) is an on-screen guide to cable programming, allowing a viewer to navigate, select, and view content by time, title, channel, genre, etc. by remote control. When used with a DVR, a viewer can locate programs they wish to view and by selecting the record option save the program to their DVR storage system for later use.

(Example interactive program guide)

Direct sales reps should possess intimate knowledge of their cable provider's IPG and remote control for both digital receiver and digital recorder units. If subscribed to cable provider service a direct sales rep can spend time at home learning the features. If a rep is not a subscriber, they should spend time using a company television to review and become familiar with the IPG and remotes.

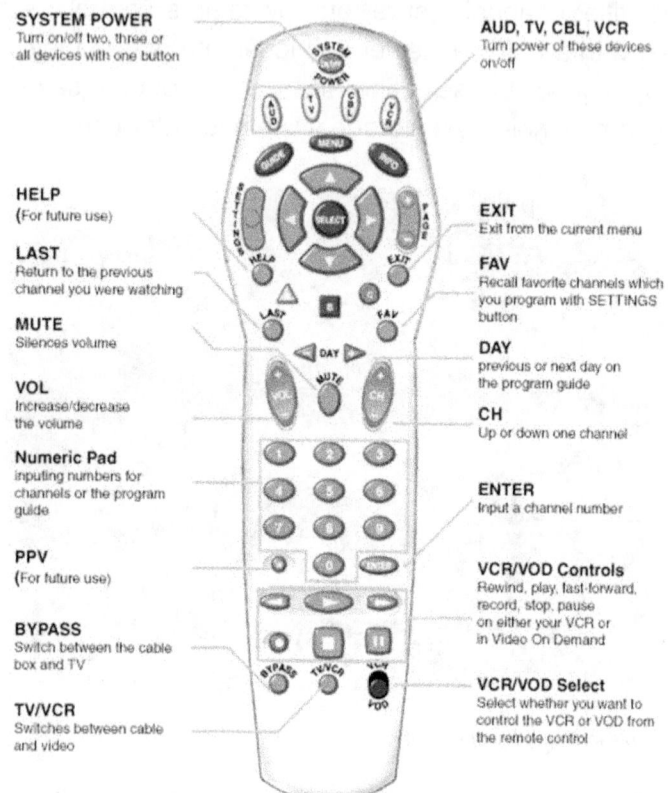

SYSTEM POWER
Turn on/off two, three or all devices with one button

AUD, TV, CBL, VCR
Turn power of these devices on/off

HELP
(For future use)

EXIT
Exit from the current menu

LAST
Return to the previous channel you were watching

FAV
Recall favorite channels which you program with SETTINGS button

MUTE
Silences volume

DAY
previous or next day on the program guide

VOL
Increase/decrease the volume

CH
Up or down one channel

Numeric Pad
inputing numbers for channels or the program guide

ENTER
Input a channel number

PPV
(For future use)

VCR/VOD Controls
Rewind, play, fast-forward, record, stop, pause on either your VCR or in Video On Demand

BYPASS
Switch between the cable box and TV

VCR/VOD Select
Select whether you want to control the VCR or VOD from the remote control

TV/VCR
Switches between cable and video

Data (Broadband Internet)

✓ Upstream & Downstream Speeds

✓ Cable Modem

Cable Internet is a form of broadband Internet access that uses the cable provider's infrastructure including digital lines and fiber optic networks, to provide access to subscribers. Similar to how DSL piggy backs on the telephone network, cable internet is layered on top of the existing cable television network infrastructure and is one of the most popular forms of residential Internet access.

Upstream & Downstream Speeds

The downstream is the speed a user can download data such as web pages, digital photographs, music and even movies. Cable broadband can provide users bit rates as high as 50 megabits per second depending on the provider. Most cable providers offer two to twenty megabits for consumers', the actual speeds can depend on a number of variables including usage of the internet and computer used. The upstream is how fast a user can upload data from their computer. Most cable users experience rates ranging from 384Kbit/s to 20Mbit/s depending on their cable provider.

Broadband cable Internet access requires a cable modem at the customer premises and a CMTS (Cable Modem Termination System) usually located at the headend. The two are connected by either coaxial cable or Hybrid Fiber Coaxial plant.

Most cable providers offer some form of Internet access only subscriptions. This means that customers can purchase the high speed service without tying it to a cable television subscription. Cable providers usually charge higher rates than if one bundles the broadband service with a video and voice subscription.

Subscribers will often use wireless routers to connect multiple computers in their home. Cable providers are witnessing the benefits in this technology and have begun to offer wireless routers within their internet packages.

(Example router)

Cable Modem

The use of cable modems enable companies to provide subscribers with high speed internet access. These modems act as a delivery system feeding power from the cable provider to a subscriber's computer.

Selling Features

- Always on, always connected
- No telephone line needed
- Voice and data from one unit and one broadband connection.
- Real-time gaming access
- Faster than dial-up accounts
- Download music and video formats within a few seconds.
- Save time and money without having to wait for content to be downloaded from the internet.

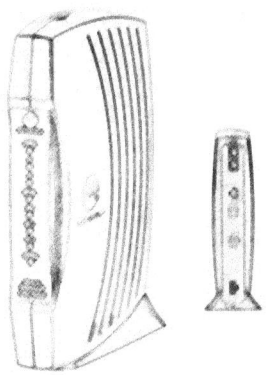

(Example modem shown)

Motorola SURFboard® Cable Modem SB5120

By utilizing the capacity of the Cable TV network, this SURFboard® SB5120 Cable Modem can access the Internet for surfing, downloading, working, shopping and gaming - at speeds up to 100 times faster than with traditional 28.8k analog phone modems*.

The use of dual cable modems, often called MTA's, enable companies to provide subscribers with high speed internet access and VoIP services. These modems act as a delivery system feeding power from the cable provider to a subscriber's computer and phone system.

*Actual speeds will vary, and are often less than the maximum possible. Upload and download speeds are affected by several factors including, but not limited to: network traffic and services offered by your cable operator or broadband service provider, computer equipment, type of server, number of connections to server, and availability of Internet router(s).

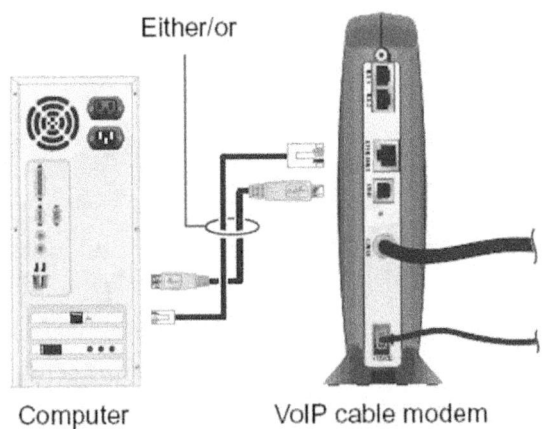

Either/or

Computer   VoIP cable modem

(Source: Motorola® www.motorola.com)

Voice (Digital Phone/VoIP)

✓ Local & Long Distance Calling

✓ Security Alarms Systems

✓ Porting Phone Numbers

Voice over Internet Protocol (VoIP) is a term for delivering voice communications over the Internet or other packet-switched networks. Other terms synonymous with VoIP included Voice over Internet (VOI), IP telephony and Internet telephony. VoIP systems usually communicate with the public switched telephone network (PSTN) allowing for transparent phone communications.

VoIP advantages include reducing communication and infrastructure costs by routing phone calls over existing data networks and avoiding duplicate network systems. VoIP transmits telephony speech as digital audio packetized in small units of typically tens of milliseconds of speech, and encapsulated in a packet stream over IP.

There is more than one option for VoIP installation. A digital VoIP can bypass all analog lines providing wireless service to subscriber's phones. A wireless phone system is set up with the base unit connected to a dual-modem (provides Internet to computer and VoIP to phone) that provides the phone system digital service.

How VoIP Works

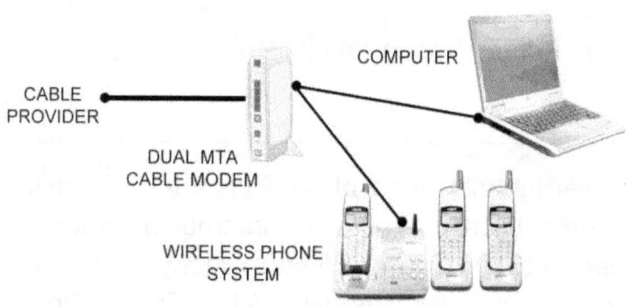

(Example basic diagram)

Analog VoIP works with a subscriber's standard phone jacks and phone lines allowing the digital signal to travel through the modem (ATA) and transmit packets via internet. This service often requires a loop to be placed at the D-mark of the subscriber's phone base.

Local & Long Distance Calling

Because of the technology cable providers can offer local and long distance calling at a considerably low rate. Many cable providers offer both local and long distance for free within their packages. Since phone calls are transmitted in digital form through internet connection, subscribers avoid paying traditional phone company fees since their service is bypassed.

Depending on the cable provider the long distance coverage may vary. Some providers offer unlimited calling to all of the United States, where some only offer to the continental US. Others may include unlimited long distance service to Mexico, Canada and Puerto Rico.

Security Alarm Systems

Not all VoIP technology supports residential security alarm systems. This information should be provided to a potential customer prior to finalizing any sale transaction. Usually technical installers will test the alarm system with the alarm company during installation, but no guarantee the system will work through the VoIP technology.

Porting Telephone Numbers

Porting a telephone number is referred to as Local number portability, (LNP) for fixed lines, which is the ability to transfer either an existing fixed-line telephone number. These numbers are assigned by a local exchange carrier (LEC) and can be reassigned to another carrier. This porting option means that a new subscriber can maintain their previous phone number when transferring to the VoIP phone service. Depending on the cable provider's infrastructure, porting capabilities may be limited. Most major MSO's now have porting capabilities nation-wide.

Pricing & Promotional Offers

✓ Product Bundles or Triple Play Offers

✓ Dish Win Back Incentives

✓ Rate Card Pricing

✓ Installation & Activation Fees

Promotional pricing is different than rate card. Cable companies provide direct sales department's special promotional pricing to assist them when trying to sell. The length of a promotion can vary. Some cable providers will offer promotions for six months or even a year, while others change promotions every thirty days.

Product Bundles or Triple Play Offers

Cable providers try and promote bundled products to provide video, voice and data to every household. By bundling the products, cable providers are able to generate more revenue than subscribers only paying for a single product, like a traditional video subscription.

Bundling consists of tying two or three cable products together usually in any combination. A bundle could consist of video and data; video and phone; or data and phone. The goal is sell all three video, voice and data, services, commonly called the triple play, to each household.

An advantage of bundling or purchasing a triple play is the subscriber savings vs. purchasing single products. Cable providers have offered six month or year-long promotions of all three services for $89 or less. A direct sales rep needs to be aware of the bundled promotions their company offers, but also the expiration date of the promotional pricing.

It is also important to know the length of the promotion. For example, a promotion may only be sold for thirty days, yet if a customer subscribes, the promotional pricing may be good for a year.

Dish Win Back Incentives

Since the primary video competitor of cable companies has been Dish Network™ and Direct TV®, sales bounties are often awarded to direct sales representatives who convert satellite customers to cable. This means cable companies will often pay additional monies to direct sales people if they can convince customers to drop their satellite service and subscribe to cable.

Some cable providers have taken the challenge a step further and provided new subscribers with credits to offset any penalties a customer may incur for early cancellation of a satellite contract. Some of these credits have been valued as high as $300 towards their cable bill.

To take advantage of these offers the direct sales rep must usually provide some form of proof that the customer was a satellite subscriber. This is usually in the form of an invoice or credit card statement. The customer credit is usually qualified with a copy of the satellite contract and penalty invoice associated.

Rate Card Pricing

Understanding the rate card pricing is important for direct sales staff. Often times a customer will ask what the price will be for the services once a promotional offer ends. Depending on the cable provider, the promotional offer may go directly to rate card pricing, or maybe a percentage increase on each product.

Most cable providers increase their rate card pricing on an annual basis and usually in January or February of each year. The average rate of increase is between 6-9% of video, voice and data services. Rate card pricing can be as high as 40% above promotional offers.

Unless bundled in a promotion, most cable companies do not offer anything but rate card for their broadcast basic or premium channel offerings.

(Example Pricing Chart)

Subscription Service	Promotional Pricing	Promotional Expiration	Standard Rate Fee
Broadcast Basic Cable	$10.21	N/A	$10.21
Expanded Basic Cable	$54.00	N/A	$54.00
Digital Tier 1	$39.99	7/1/2009	$56.00
Digital Tier 2	$49.00	7/1/2009	$65.00
Digital Tier 3	$59.00	7/1/2009	$79.00
5MB Broadband	$35.00	3/30/2009	$45.00
10MB Broadband	$55.00	N/A	$55.00
VoIP Phone Service	$19.99	5/31/2009	$38.00
Triple Play Offer *Digital Tier 1, 5MB Broadband & VoIP for $99.00* *Offer Expires 3/31/2009*			

Depending on location and franchise agreements broadcast basic charges vary. Certain cities or geographical areas within a cable provider's footprint can have different rates for their basic cable service. This can be important for direct sales representatives selling basic cable service in those locations to avoid misquoting. To attempt to eliminate confusion some cable providers will offer expanded basic for the same rate across the board, even if the broadcast basic is dollars higher in specific locations.

Installation & Activation Fees

Each cable provider has their own set of rules when it comes to installation or activation fees. Some companies provide free installation and waive activation fees for their direct sales department to facilitate the impulse purchase.

Of course the specifics fluctuate regarding how many outlets are covered in the free installation or if there are additional charges to wall fish. It's imperative that direct sales people educate themselves on the amount of outlets covered and what an additional outlet would cost. With technical training a direct sales rep can estimate if a wall fish will be needed and let the customer know that an additional cost may be incurred.

The best way a direct sales rep can handle this is by explaining to the customer the possibility of the additional charges, but not quoting them the amount. This should be covered by the installer prior to doing any work inside the customer's home.

Gaining Competitor Knowledge

✓ Who Is the Competition?

✓ Collecting Competitive Collateral

✓ Online Research

✓ Dissecting Competitive Offers

The old adage "keep your friends close and your enemies closer" is true when it come to understanding competitive knowledge. To gain a competitive edge a direct sales representative must know as much about the competitor as they do about their own company. This can be very challenging since technology advancements appear frequently, thus changing products and services offered.

Who Is The Competition?

The first step in gaining competitive knowledge is to identifying the competition. Who is the competition? What do they offer? Where do they provide services? How competitive is their service? How competitive is their pricing?

Method: Satellite　　　　　　　　　　Direct TV®
Services: Video
Coverage: Nation-wide coverage in both
rural and urban markets.

Direct TV® is a national satellite video provider with multiple high definition channel offerings. The company possesses exclusivity of the Sunday Ticket, which offers every National Football League game televised. The company also provides up to one hundred high definition channels when local, regional and national networks are included. Digital video recorders may also be provided through this service. Video packages range in price from approximately $30 to $100.

Method: Satellite　　　　　　　　　Dish Network™
Services: Video
Coverage: Nation-wide coverage in both
rural and urban markets.

Dish Network™ is a national satellite video provider with over one hundred high definition channel offerings when local, regional and national networks are included. The company provides premium channels, sporting events and major network programming. Digital video recorders may also be provided through this service. Video packages range in price from approximately $30 to $100.

Method: Fiber   AT&T U-verse
Services: Video, voice and data
Coverage: Nation-wide with focused on
major markets.

AT&T U-verse provides video, voice and data with over 75 high definition channels, VOD and DVR. The internet service offers download speeds of up to 18Mbs. Digital video recorders may also be provided through this service. Bundle packs range from $69 for 2 products to $145 for three product offers. In addition to video, voice and data offerings, AT&T may also offer their cellular phone service within their U-verse packages.

Method: Fiber   Verizon FiOS
Services: Video, voice and data
Coverage: Nation-wide with focused on
major markets.

Verizon FiOS provides video, voice and data with up to 100 high definition channels, VOD and DVR. The internet service offers download speeds of up to 30-50Mbs depending on area. Digital video recorders may also be provided through this service. Video packages starting at $47 and Triple play packages start at $79 a month. In addition to video, voice and data offerings, may also offer their cellular phone service within their Verizon packages.

Once the information is collected a comparison can be made of products and services offered. The comparison should view not only price, but also features available on all areas of service including video, voice and data.

By comparing the competition side by side with the cable provider offering, a direct sales representative can determine a sales strategy to compete against each competitor. This knowledge is crucial when in discussion with potential customers. Customers may ask about how a cable company stacks up against the competition.

Collecting Competitive Collateral

Cable competitors often market using direct mail sent directly to consumers' homes. Mailers can also be embedded in newspapers similar to direct mail collateral. Direct sales reps should collect as much of this material as they can when presented during field sales.

Radio and television commercials are also a good way to stay in sync with what offer the competitor's are providing consumers. Brochures and handouts with competitive information may also be located at electronic stores and kiosks at local malls.

This information is valuable because the direct sales rep can now use the competitive information within their sales strategy. The information should also be shared with their supervisor or manager to review. This can have a significant impact on how to counteract competitive offers.

Online Research

Using the internet as away to stay in touch with the competition can prove valuable for direct sales people. In addition to the major satellite providers and depending on markets, fiber providers, there are also additional companies to seek out. These include internet service providers, telephone companies, and competitive cable providers if in a cable overlay market.

Below is a list of websites of some major cable competitors that provide promotional information online.

www.directv.com	*www.dishnetwork.com*
www.verizon.com (FiOS)	*www.att.com (U-verse)*
www.qwest.com	*www.tdstelecom.com*
www.hughesnet.com	*www.wildblue.com*
www.vonage.com	*www.skype.com*
www.aol.com	*www.netzero.net*

Dissecting Competitive Offers

Understanding both the competition strength and weakness can help overcome the loss of a sale. This can be accomplished by breaking down or dissecting the service and offer of each competitor. By making a list, a direct sales rep can study and commit to memory the strengths and weaknesses each competitor poses.

Some criteria to include in comparison:

- Pricing for low to high video offering
- Programming and HD channels offered
- Exclusive Programming (Cable Access)
- Download & upload speeds
- Data transfer caps
- Long distance limitations
- Cost for service after promotion
- Locally provided customer service
- Installation or activation fees
- Cost for digital receiver, DVR or modem
- Contracts or penalty fees
- Service charges if service is interrupted

Chapter review

This section is to determine the knowledge gained from the previous chapter. If a direct sales rep is unable to provide an answer to any of the questions, they should make note and research to locate the correct information.

Product Knowledge Quiz

1. How much is broadcast basic cable service?

   _____

2. How many digital tiers can be offered to subscribers?

   _____

3. Can a premium channel be sold to a basic analog customer?

   _____

4. How much is HBO separate from a package?

   _____

5. How many HD channels are offered?

_____

6. Which HD Channels are offered in each package?

_____

_____

_____

_____

_____

_____

_____

_____

7. Does a customer need a special digital receiver to view the HD programming?

_____

8. How many types of HD digital receivers can be offered to a customer? List them.

_____

_____

9. What is the monthly fee for a DVR?

_____

10. How much for an additional DVR?

_____

11. Will the customer be able to wirelessly receive signal to each home computer?

_____

12. How fast is the download speed?

_____

13. Is there a cap on downloading files such as music and movies?

_____

14. Will the cable internet work with any computer?

_____

15. Can a subscriber port their number to the new cable phone system?

_____

16. Is there a fee associated with phone porting? If so, how much is the cost?

_____

17. What areas of the United States can a subscriber call without incurring long distance charges?

_____

18. If a subscriber calls outside the free long distance range, how much will they be charged each minute?

_____

19. Will the cable digital phone system work with a "Life Alert" system?

_____

20. If electricity goes out of a subscriber home will they still have access to their digital phone system?

_____

21. What video package is offered with the triple play?

_____

22. How much is the triple play offer and how long is the promotion?

_____

23. Can a subscriber elect to bundle two products?

_____

24. Is there a contract associated with the subscriber service(s)?

_____

25. What cable access programs are available?

_____

Field Process Knowledge
Comprehensive Description of Responsibilities

- ✓ Credit Scoring

- ✓ Processing a Sales Order

- ✓ Schedule Installation

- ✓ Review Sales Order

Direct sales representatives are expected to carry out an array of tasks when selling in the field. Each cable provider has specific policies and procedures that are required to be followed. These are guidelines that help protect the direct sales rep, customer and company. In addition, these guidelines offer support and assist in helping direct sales reps achieve their sales goals.

Credit Scoring
Cable providers use credit scoring as means of protecting their company assets. Equipment such as digital receivers, digital video recorders and modems can cost hundreds of dollars. By establishing a credit scoring

procedure cable companies can shed light on a subscriber's bill payment history.

Credit scoring agencies such as Equifax®, TransUnion®, and Experian, are leveraged to provide cable companies with this information. Some cable providers will use all three of these agencies. The intent is to determine the amount of risk a provider may associate with a subscriber depending on their credit score.

Identification Check

To perform a credit score through these agencies a subscriber's social security number must be provided. In addition, cable providers require most direct sales reps to confirm a prospects identity with both a social security card and state issued identification card or driver's license. Depending on the provider, these confirmations can be as simple as a direct sales representative's acknowledgment of viewing the information, or required to submit photocopies of the identification when turning in sales orders.

Historically cable companies have experienced a high volume of identity fraud with past subscribers. Individuals would provide cable companies with false names, social security numbers and other forms of identification. In addition to the sales review process, most cable providers also require identification to be shown to an installation technician prior to install.

Over the years the cable companies have strengthened their confirmation process by taking additional steps to prevent or reduce identity fraud from occurring. If a direct sales representative is faced with a potential customer who refuses to show identification they should contact their supervisor prior to placing a sales order. Although some customers are concerned with showing their identification for legitimate reasons, there are others who refuse because of owing past due or fear of low credit scoring.

Past Due Balance

With the information provided for running credit scores a cable company also checks for any past history of the prospect. Sometimes the information provided is cross referenced through software that shows a past due amount owed by the prospect from a prior service date. This means the prospect a direct sales rep is attempting to sell has been a customer in the past. If a past due amount is showing in the customer history there are several possibilities as to why the amount is posted to an account.

The customer could have voluntarily asked to disconnect service, yet didn't pay their final bill. The customer could have voluntarily asked to disconnect service, yet failed to return company equipment which incurred charges on their account. Some equipment such as DVR's can post amounts as high as $500. The customer could have been disconnected because of non-payment and the amount was never collected.

Depending on the length of time between disconnect and re-establishing contact a direct sales rep may need to investigate with the prior customer to establish reasoning for any past due activity on account.

Charges Associated with Credit Score

To offset the risk of churn or no-pay disconnects, cable providers often associate an installation and/or activation fee to subscribers who return a low credit score. These fees are usually required prior to installation of any subscriber service.

Amnesty Programs

To increase subscriber base some cable providers will institute an amnesty program. These programs have been designed as a way for cable providers to reach out to past customers whom have been disconnected due to non-payment. Amnesty allows the former customers with past debt the ability to subscribe to cable services.

There are different variations of the amnesty program. Some include restricting past debt customers to providing basic only service until past due is paid in full. This enables past debt customers to still subscribe to service while the cable provider eliminates risk from loss of digital equipment. Other programs will erase a portion or entire debt depending on criteria such as amount owed or time elapsed.

Processing a Sales Order

Not every cable provider is the same when it comes to processing sales orders. Some companies require a customer's signature on every order. Some cable companies provide internet order forms for their reps vs. carbon copy forms. The following pages include processes used by most major cable providers, but each direct sales rep should check with their supervisor to confirm their company procedures.

Sales Order Forms

Sales order forms are provided as a guide to direct sales reps to ensure that all needed information is completed. The forms also act as confirmation to both the cable provider and subscriber of services requested. Sales order forms provide areas of information to be completed including customer name, address, phone number as well as services ordered, pricing and installation date and time.

Direct sales representatives should make sure that all of the information on a sales order form is completed in full. It is also important that the forms are legible for later reference. Sales orders are often in duplicate or triplicate form so copies can be separated and distributed to specific locations including sales department, technical operations and customer.

Calling In Sales Orders

Since most MSO's use credit scoring, a sales support center is usually made available. These support centers often provide a dedicated phone number for direct sales. The support center primarily focuses on supporting direct sales orders by processing credit scoring, sales order entry and scheduling availability.

Depending on the size and volume of the support center and demand for support, there may be stress placed on time per call. In these cases companies usually require that a direct sales rep have all the information completed on a sales order prior to calling in an order. This practice can help expedite orders and conserve time for each order processed.

Accepting Payment

Methods of payment are determined by each cable provider. Major credit cards, check and cash are the primary forms used. Some companies and or divisions of companies have strict policies requiring direct sales representatives to only accept checks and/or process credit cards as forms of payment. This eliminates the chance of misplacing customer cash from a transaction.

A good practice is to write the check number somewhere visible on each sales order form for tracking.

Schedule Installation

Prior to requesting an installation date a direct sales rep should have the customer provide a couple dates and times they could be available. This saves time and confusion when trying schedule out. Once a direct sales rep has these dates they should be able to call a support center and get an order scheduled. Some cable providers have same day or instant installs programs in place. This enables a direct sales rep to have a new subscriber installed the same day of the sale.

Cable technicians usually perform installations from a work order. These work orders include the services a customer ordered, number of outlets to be activated and any notes regarding special requests. A direct sales rep should include any notes that a customer requests when calling in the sale. This could include requesting that the technician call ahead prior to arrival; or ask that they not parking in a driveway, etc.. This type of communication can assist the technician greatly when preparing for an install.

Review Order

Whether a sale is conducted within a customer's home or over the phone it's critical to review prior to finalizing. This practice can help prevent customer service issues and scheduling conflicts in the future.

Information that should be reviewed with each customer sale includes:

- Contact Information
- Subscription Services
- Pricing
- Number of Outlets
- Customer Signature
- Confirm Payment & COD
- Installation Date & Time
- Customer Copy Provided

Follow Up

Direct sales reps should track their completed installs. This process allows them to contact their new customers and confirm the installation occurred and that they're satisfied with their new services. It is also an opportune time to request a referral for new business.

Managing Turf (Nodes)

✓ Identifying Sales Territory

✓ SFU & MDU

✓ Reviewing Street Sheets

✓ Contact Ratio

Each cable company has specific territories that they can provide services to through their cable plant. These areas are broken up into nodes. Some nodes can be quite large and are broken down further into node legs. The nodes are provided power by way of either trunk and feeder cable with amplifiers, or in new or rebuilt systems the use of fiber optic lines run from the headend.

Nodes are designed to provide service to homes passed. Usually a node is comprised of homes between the amounts of 500 and 1000. A sales representative's focus is to work within a node to sell video, voice and data services to homes that are not currently active subscribers; or upgrade current subscribers with additional services.

Identify Sales Territory

Direct sales representatives' work either in an assigned area comprised of specific nodes, or in a sweeper format. An assigned territory representative is designated to sell within a confined geographic location. All homes passed within this location usually belong to the assigned rep and may include both SFU (single family units) and MDU (multi-dwelling units) opportunities.

A sweeper, often referred to as a floater, usually roams from node to node working every home passed. A sweeper may work multiple nodes at a given time. The purpose of a sweeper is to simply establish as much contact as possible with the node currently worked.

SFU (Single Family Units)

SFU, or single family unit, is classified as a home or residence occupied by an individual or family. Although usually classified as a home owner, a SFU could also be a rental home. Cable companies see greater value with SFU subscribers' because of the lower amount of churn. Since most SFU's are home owners the risk of them moving as often as a subscriber who lives in an apartment complex is far less, thus sustaining greater customer retention.

MDU (Multi-Dwelling Units)

MDU, or multi-dwelling unit, is classified as multiple family housing units such as a duplex, townhouse or apartment complex. Cable companies often pay less commission on these types of subscriber sales because they historically are considered more transient and pose a greater risk of churn than those subscribers residing in a SFU.

Reviewing Street Sheets

Street sheets, often referred to as turf sheets or green bar, can provide direct sales representatives with both active and inactive customer information. Within each street sheet names, addresses, telephone numbers and classification codes designating active, never and former customer statuses should be provided. Active customers listed should include the services they're currently subscribed to differenciate when attempting a sales upgrade.

Contact Ratio

A contact ratio is determined by how many attempts a direct sales rep makes by knocking doors when canvassing an area vs. the amount of contacts established.

One of the most successful practices to increase contact rates is the "three attempt rule". Successful direct sales representatives will try to establish contact at first during the day. This allows them to read their street sheets and see the addresses in the daylight and become familiar with their territory.

If contact is not established an attempt is then made during the evening usually after 5pm. If again contact is still not established, a representative will make one final attempt at contact during a Saturday. By practicing the "three attempt rule" a direct sales representative can generate a higher contact ratio, and in return produce higher sales. This method of territory management is also valuable in not burning through turf.

Street Sheet

Rockford/Dixon Printed 2/23/2005
Node Rockford 7A

Customer Address	Customer Phone	Code	Service Type	Service Date	
Roger Baumgardener 1287 Venus St. Machesney Park, IL 61115	815-555-1212	A	Basic Classic Digital 2.0 BB Insight 10.0	08/21/1997	12 AUDIT NH
1308 Venus Street Machesney Park, IL 61115	Unknown	N			
Bill Smull 1309 Venus Street Machesney Park, IL 61115	815-555-2365	A	BB Insight 10.0	11/04/2002	12 AUDIT Pres Callback 2/24 7pm
Patrice Givens 1310 Venus Street Machesney Park, IL 61115	000-000-0000	F			12:30 AUDIT Pres Sale Dish Winback B/C/BB

EXAMPLE

Technical Comprehension

✓ Cable Infrastructure

✓ Installer Ride Day

✓ Blind Audit Process

Today cable television systems deliver entertainment video, high speed internet and digital phone service to consumers' homes. In addition to the video, voice and data, many cable systems provide extended services, such as Video-on-Demand. While the capabilities of cable systems have been enhanced, cable systems have evolved into a hybrid-fiber coax (HFC) structure.

The cable television architecture consists of five major components including the headend; optical fiber; feeder cable; drop cable; and terminal equipment.

Cable Infrastructure

Cable programming content is received and processed at the headend. A network programmer transmits a television signal through the air from a satellite, microwave, or local television antenna to the headend. They may also send the content by a direct fiber link from the studio. The content received is then modulated to become a radio frequency (RF) signal that is part of a frequency spectrum. The headend then assigns each signal a unique channel frequency, which occupies a unique portion of the spectrum. The combined signals then distribute content from providers and are then transmitted through the cable network to homes.

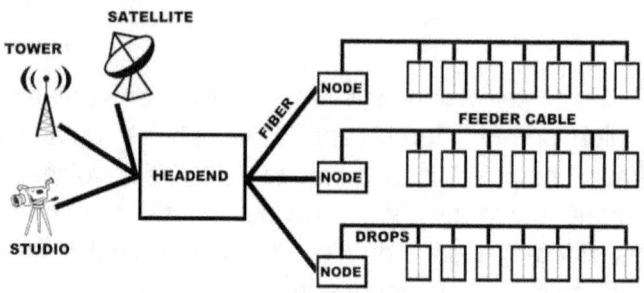

In the early day's trunk, feeder, and drop cables were how subscribers received their service. Today's trunk cables and amplifiers are replaced by single optical fiber lines. The fiber optics transmits RF energy by way of light reflecting down a glass fiber. This reduces noise and distortion in the cable plant. The process also eliminates the need for amplifiers. With HFC architecture, a single fiber is run directly from the headend to an optical node in a neighborhood. The node converts the optical signal back to RF signals and the local neighborhood part of the cable plant distributes the RF signals the same as before. Nodes are spaced to serve a neighborhood with 500 to 1000 homes passed by the plant.

Another benefit of the HFC architecture is that it enables the cable plant to reliably deliver signals that originate in subscribers homes and relays back to the headend. This two-way capability enables interactive audio, video and data services. Because of the popularity in cable over the last fifty years many homes have been installed in the past and are wired for cable service. MSO's now run cable underground vs. using telephone poles like years past. When a customer purchases cable and the home has never had the service prior, or have had cable trenched, the cable installer will run a drop cable from a tap on a feeder cable into the subscriber's home. The drop cable is then connected to digital equipment inside the home. The terminal equipment processes the cable signals and enables subscribers to view, record, and interact with the services.

Installer Ride Day

To better understand the technical process of how cable works at the subscribers' home, ride days are implemented within sales training programs. These ride days enable a direct sales rep to see first-hand what is entailed in a video, voice and/or data installation.

During a ride day with a technician or installer a direct sales representative should observe a variety of processes including:

- Performing Audits
- Hot Taps
- Disconnects (Analog)
- Video, Voice & Data Installation

The experience should provide knowledge on wall fishing, outlet installation, activations, testing and other aspects of a professional cable installation. If a multi-dwelling unit is scheduled during the ride day, a direct sales representative can also learn the hot tap process used when connecting and disconnecting apartment complexes.

The installer ride day purpose is to educate the direct sales rep so they can understand the install process and also provide knowledge to decrease truck rolls or customer services issues. By having a technical understanding the direct sales representative should walk away from the experience knowing both the possibilities and limitations of the service they sell.

Blind Audit Process

The blind audit process is a practice enabling a direct sales representative to review homes passed on a street sheet and identify, locate and resolve the use of unauthorized cable service.

By reviewed streets sheets a direct sales representative can identify which services a subscriber is being charged. They can then review the connection from the drop to the home and see what type of filter or connector is issued to trap out services the subscriber is not being charged.

For example, if a direct sales representative locates a home on their street sheet that is currently charged for basic analog cable, yet they are unable to locate the connector that traps a higher end service (family, classic, etc.), the subscriber may be receiving unauthorized programming.

Each cable system has a set of procedures on how to identify and handle unauthorized service. The following is a suggested process which prompts the direct sales rep to contact their cable provider and confirm the services in billing. If confirmation is obtained an SRO (service request order) can be placed to schedule a technician to review and trap the additional services from entering the subscribers' home.

One sales tip is for the direct sales representative to attempt contact and educate the customer on the unauthorized service. This allows the direct sales representative to possibly upgrade the customer and prevents the customer from losing additional programming.

Sales Organization

✓ Building a Hot List

✓ Sales Collateral

✓ Presentation & Preparation

To be successful a direct sales representative must possess both organizational skills and manage their time effectively. This section covers how to stay organized with sales materials and marketing collateral. It also covers how a direct sales representative manages their day with appointments, leads and other contacts.

Preparation is the key to organization. The better prepared a direct sales representative is with their materials and time, the better they will be prepared for customer interaction and selling.

Each day a direct sales representative must possess all material needed to succeed and leverage their time in the field wisely. There are only so many hours in the day, wasting this time because of lack of organization will have a negative effect on sales.

Building a Hot List

By maintaining a *hot list* a sales representative arms themselves with an organized list used to grow sales.

A *hot list* is comprised of potential customers contacted that have expressed some interest in product offers. These are essentially leads that can be called back on for conversion to become new customers.

There are a variety of ways to create or manage a *hot list* but should all include certain pertinent information.

- Prospect name
- Address
- Phone number
- Date of contact
- Products of interest
- Call Back Date & Time

Some variations of the *hot list* may only include phone numbers to contact so a direct sales representative may conserve time and fuel. A *hot list* may also be structured by a specific product so the list is easier to manage.

To qualify whether a contact should be on a *hot list* is decided by each individual direct sales representative. Some direct sales representative may wish for the prospect to provide a verbal acknowledgement to purchase prior to being added to their list.

(Example Hot List 1)

Date	Name	Address	City	Phone
8/12/08	Tom Rain	123 Main	Lincoln	555-4121
Best Time To Contact		**Product Of Interest**		
Saturday AM		Basic video and VoIP service		
Date	Name	Address	City	Phone
8/12/08	Jane Bell	212 4th	Lincoln	555-9825
Best Time To Contact		**Product Of Interest**		
Weekday evenings		Triple play with HBO		

(Example Hot List 2)

Broadband Leads		
Date	**Name**	**Phone**
8/12/08	Katherine Brown	555-4530
8/12/08	Roger Dolby	555-7771
8/12/08	Maria Gomez	555-0085
8/13/08	Diane Voss	555-3367
VoIP Leads		
Date	**Name**	**Phone**
8/12/08	Jason Cusack	555-9833

Others may follow a gut instinct, and add people that they feel will purchase after a specific timeframe. The timeframe may have relevance to financial situation, current provider contract or discussion with spouse.

A suggestion would be to have the *hot list* maintained in a protective folder or three-ring binder and always kept in vehicle for ease of access.

To manage a *hot list* successfully it must be updated daily and referenced to call upon regularly. The longer a direct sales representative waits to call upon a lead or prospect, the greater the chances they will lose interest or sign up with a competitor.

Sales Collateral

The use of sales materials is a crucial tool used to communicate the company's product offering. Sales collateral comes in many different forms including direct mailers, radio and television commercials, billboards and brochures.

In direct sales, collateral is vital too, providing the direct sales representative a method of disseminating marketing information to potential subscribers. Direct sales collateral may include brochures, business cards, door hangers or other marketing leave behinds.

Channel Lineup

A cable channel lineup is the most valuable form of collateral available when relating to video offering. The programming offered in the Channel Lineup is what separates cable companies from satellite providers such as Dish Network® and Direct TV®.

Channel lineup cards may be formatted in different ways depending on the cable company. There are theme-based cards, analog vs. digital separated cards, and plain numeric format offerings.

It is important for a direct sales representative to become familiar with the lineup card(s) used in their sales area and memorize all of the channels available. This includes basic, standard, premium, HD (high definition) and digital channels.

Since many cable providers can offer hundreds of channels depending on the package, this may be time consuming. Depending on the package offered, channels will be different. It is important to keep updated with which channels are offered in specific packages. It is equally important to know which channels and packages are offered in HD.

Direct sales representatives should have an abundance of channel lineup cards at their disposal. It is difficult to offer video related products if one can't show a prospect what programming is offered.

Brochures

Another form of sales material used by direct sales representative is brochures. Brochures can contain information such as benefits, features and pricing on products offered.

Brochures are often used to promote a specific product or service or upgrade that a cable company is rolling out such as VoIP, Broadband Boost or additional HD programming. Some brochures are also used as informational enhancements to educate the consumer of their product offering.

By reviewing the brochures a direct sales representative can also educate themselves on the features and benefits offered. This can then be used during the sales process to peak the prospects curiosity and generate questions of interest.

Note: The following is an example Channel Lineup card used in 2007 by Insight Communications.

THEME-BASED DIGITAL CHANNEL LINEUP

ENTERTAINMENT

106 USA Network
109 TBS
112 TNT
115 WGN
116 FX
121 Lifetime
124 Lifetime Real Women
125 WE: Women's Entertainment
127 SOAPnet
128 Oxygen
133 E! Entertainment
136 Style
141 Spike TV
142 GSN
143 G4
148 Comedy Central
151 Fox Reality Channel
156 Sci-Fi Channel
158 A&E
161 Court TV
166 BET
167 TV One
173 BBC America
181 Bravo
182 AmericanLife TV

LIFE & HOME

206 HGTV
209 Fine Living
211 Food Network
214 DIY Network
217 TLC
221 Discovery Home
224 Discovery Health
229 Lime
240 QVC
241 Home Shopping Network
242 ShopNBC
243 Jewelry Television
244 ICN

FAMILY

256 TV Land
257 ABC Family
260 Hallmark Channel
275 EWTN
276 i-LifeTV
277 Trinity Broadcasting Network
282 TLN-51 Rockford

KIDS

306 Nickelodeon
307 Nick Too
308 Nick GAS
309 Nick Toons
315 Disney Channel
317 Toon Disney
325 Cartoon Network
335 Noggin
336 PBS KIDS Sprout
338 Discovery Kids

MULTICULTURAL

357 Univision
358 Telemundo
361 TV Chile
362 Latin TV
363 Enlace
364 Latele Novela
365 La Familia Network
366 Toon Disney en Español
367 VeneMovies
369 CNN en Español
371 Discovery en Español
372 History Channel en Español
373 ESPN Deportes
374 Fox Sports en Español
375 Cine Latino
376 Cine Mexicano
377 HBO Latino
379 Canal 52 MX
380 mun2
381 Puma TV
383 MTV Español
390 AZN Television

NEWS & DOCUMENTARIES

406 Fox News Channel
407 CNN
409 CNN Headline News
411 Bloomberg
412 CNBC
413 CNBC World
414 MSNBC
430 The Weather Channel
445 C-SPAN
446 C-SPAN 2
447 C-SPAN 3
450 National Geographic
453 Travel Channel

NEWS & DOCUMENTARIES (CONT'D)

455 Animal Planet
461 Discovery Channel
464 The Science Channel
471 Discovery Times
482 The Biography Channel
483 The History Channel
485 History International
486 Military Channel

SPORTS

506 ESPN
509 ESPN2
512 ESPN Classic
513 ESPNEWS
514 ESPNU
522 Comcast SportsNet
524 Comcast Sportsnet Plus/IHSA
531 CSTV
533 Fox College Sports Atlantic
534 Fox College Sports Central
535 Fox College Sports Pacific
547 NFL Network
549 Versus (formerly Outdoor Life)
551 Speed Channel
553 The Outdoor Channel
555 Fox Soccer Channel
557 Tennis Channel
558 The Golf Channel
563 TVG
564 Horse Racing Television
581 ESPN Sports Pay-Per-View 1
582 ESPN Sports Pay-Per-View 2
583 ESPN Sports Pay-Per-View 3
584 ESPN Sports Pay-Per-View 4
585 ESPN Sports Pay-Per-View 5
586 ESPN Sports Pay-Per-View 6

MOVIES

607 Fox Movie Channel
608 Turner Classic Movies
610 AMC
611 Lifetime Movie Network
612 Independent Film Channel
614 Sundance Channel
616 Sundance Channel (West)
630 Encore
633 Encore (West)
634 Encore Warn
635 Encore Action

Please see Exceptions and Disclaimers Below:
HDTV set, Basic Service, HD receiver (or Insight CableCard) required to receive all HD channels. Subscription to Classic service and atleast 1 Digital Programming Pak (or Digital Standard/Choice) is also required to receive MHD, TNT, in HD and ESPN2 HD. Not all programming available in all areas.

Check out Channel 9!

MOVIES (CONT'D)

636 Encore Action (West)
637 Encore Drama
638 Encore Drama (West)
639 Encore Love
640 Encore Love (West)
641 Encore Mystery
642 Encore Mystery (West)
643 Encore Westerns
644 Encore Westerns (West)
650 Starz
653 Starz (West)
654 Starz Edge
657 Starz Kids & Family
659 Starz Cinema
661 Starz InBlack
664 Starz Comedy
790 HBO
704 HBO2
706 HBO Zone
707 HBO Latino
709 HBO Signature
712 HBO Family
714 HBO Comedy
730 Cinemax
734 MoreMAX
736 ActionMAX
738 ThrillerMAX
750 Showtime
753 Showtime (West)
755 Showtime Too
756 Showtime Too (West)
757 Showtime Showcase
758 Showtime Showcase (West)
759 Showtime Extreme
760 Showtime Extreme (West)
780 FLIX
781 FLIX (West)
785 The Movie Channel
786 The Movie Channel (West)
787 The Movie Channel Xtra
788 The Movie Channel Xtra (West)

MUSIC

806 MTV
808 MTV2
809 MTV Hits
810 MTV Jams
811 MTV Español
814 VH1

for On Demand TV

MUSIC (CONT'D)

815 VH1 Classic
816 VH1 Soul
819 BET Jazz
821 CMT
822 CMT Pure Country
823 GAC
826 Fuse
842 Latin Contemporary
843 Fiesta Tropical
844 Rock 'en Español
845 Latin Jazz
846 Regional Mexican
847 Tejano
848 Salsa
849 Musica de las Americas
850 Showcase
851 Today's Country
852 Classic Country
853 Bluegrass
854 R&B and Hip-Hop
855 Classic R&B
856 Smooth R&B
857 R&B Hits
858 Rap
859 Metal
860 Rock
861 Arena Rock
862 Classic Rock
863 Alternative
864 Retro-Active
865 Electronica
866 Dance
867 Adult Alternative
868 Soft Rock
869 Hit List
870 Party Favorites
871 90s
872 80s
873 70s
874 Solid Gold Oldies
875 Singers & Standards
876 Big Band & Swing
877 Easy Listening
878 Smooth Jazz
879 Jazz
880 Blues
881 Reggae
882 Soundscapes
883 Classical Masterpieces
884 Opera
885 Light Classical
886 Show Tunes

MUSIC (CONT'D)

887 Contemporary Christian
888 Gospel
889 Radio Disney
890 Sounds of the Seasons
891 Musica Urbana
892 Salsa y Merengue
893 Rock 'en Español
894 Pop Latino
895 Mexicana
896 Americana

HDTV

906 WREX HD (NBC)
908 WTVO HD (ABC)
912 WIFR HD (CBS)
923 ESPN HD
924 ESPN2 HD
925 TNT in HD
928 HDNet
935 Discovery HD Theater
937 Universal HD
945 MHD
949 HDNet Movies
952 HBO HD
954 Showtime HD

PAY-PER-VIEW

961 Hot Choice
973 IN DEMAND Pay-Per-View 1
974 IN DEMAND Pay-Per-View 2
975 IN DEMAND Pay-Per-View 3
976 IN DEMAND Pay-Per-View 4
977 IN DEMAND Pay-Per-View 5
978 IN DEMAND Pay-Per-View 6
987 ESPN Sports Pay-Per-View 1
988 ESPN Sports Pay-Per-View 2
989 ESPN Sports Pay-Per-View 3
990 ESPN Sports Pay-Per-View 4
991 ESPN Sports Pay-Per-View 5
992 ESPN Sports Pay-Per-View 6

KEY

n   Digital Choice
n   Audio Music
n   HD
n   HD Pak
n   Premium / PPV

Sales brochures are excellent leave behinds for prospects to review with their family prior to making a buying decision. A direct sales representative should try and schedule an appointment to visit and re-evaluate the product offer when leaving the prospect with a brochure to review.

Usually brochures are in short demand because they often possess a short life cycle. Like the channel lineup, a direct sales representative should have a solid amount of brochures, yet use sparingly to those they feel confident will buy. Or leverage as a tool to gain additional appointments.

Door Hangers vs. Sticky Notes

The longtime battle to use either the door hanger or the sticky note as a leave behind for missed contacts rages on. There are benefits in using both. The door hanger can often be printed in full color press with a heavier stock for durability, while the sticky pad can be a more friendly material if direct sales representative wish to stamp their contact information. The sticky note is usually easier to handle and carry from door to door.

The door hanger usually is a larger format and can offer printed information on both sides. This comes in handy when printing information in both English and Spanish.

The downsides include both formats losing their position from a door due to wind or other weather related elements. Although both formats can be successful, the goal is to establish contact with a consumer so the leave behind such as the door hanger or sticky note is not needed.

Personalized Handouts

By personalizing a flyer or handout a direct sales representative can separate themselves from the other marketing materials. A direct sales rep needs to personalize their materials to not get lost with other company marketing efforts. By adding their cell phone and providing promotional information and pricing the rep can designate themselves as the point of contact, thus increasing the chance to gain the sale.

Most direct sales representatives are only paid on sales installed. If a rep approaches a prospect, establishes contact and educates them on the product offering they're not always guaranteed a sale. If the prospect in return calls a company sales line, customer service center or signs up through a walk-in payment center, the direct sales representative will not get credit for the sale.

Because of this fact, personalization is a must when distributing any sales material. If using a personalized flyer or handout, a direct sales representative should have

approved prior to printing and distributing. Usually a
company sales manager is the approving source.

Note: Example of personalized direct sales flyer.

Cable Povider Name & Logo

As your local neighborhood representative I'm authorized to offer you some
amazing offers from Insight Communications. Simply select a package that best
fits you and call me directly for more information or to take advantage of the
following offers.

Down to Basics
Broadcast Basic Cable only $8 a month

Double your Deal
Broadcast Basic Cable and High-Speed Broadband Internet $38 a month
Basic/Classic cable, Digital Service, (1 year FREE Showtime), and High-Speed
Broadband Internet $75 a month

Bundled Three Product Offer
Basic/Classic cable, Digital Service, (1 year FREE Showtime), and High-Speed
Broadband Internet with UNLIMITED Long Distance Phone Service $105 a
month

In addition, we offer:

- FREE Installation!* (Some restrictions may apply)
- ½ OFF 1st Month Service!
- NO CONTRACTS! Insight will even credit you up to $300 to get you out of
  your current Satellite contract and $100 for your current DSL contract plus
  give you 1 year of FREE Showtime & Encore!
- Have an old bill? Call me for help!
- Refer a friend and you'll receive $10 off your cable bill

Please note that you MUST contact me directly to receive the above special
offers. As your neighborhood representative I'm authorized as a company
specialist and the offer is not valid through our call-in or walk-in centers.

To take advantage of these offers call me today!

Best regards,
Wayne

Presentation & Preparation

Preparing for the work day is important to any direct sales representative. Their appearance should be neat and hygiene excellent. A door to door sales person deals with people each day and often is called upon to be in a prospect's home. A prospect judges a company and their offer by who provides them the information. This is a direct reflection on the sales person. By being presentable a direct sales representative has a greater chance of engaging a prospect.

A direct sales representative should wear a clean and wrinkle free shirt, sweatshirt, and/or jacket or coat that identifies them as a cable company employee. In addition, they should also wear clean and pressed slacks. If jeans are worn there should be no tears or worn appearance. A direct sales representative should also have an identification badge that shows their picture, their name, title, cable company name and logo.

Other preparations to consider include vehicle is fueled and clean. Cell phone battery is charged and ready for use. Contact numbers are available and stored in a clipboard or briefcase.

If a cable company requires a direct sales representative to turn money collected in from prior day sales, make sure it is accounted for and matching sales orders.

Material Preparation

In door to door sales, representatives must have materials available to provide to prospects. Prior to starting each day a representative should ensure they have all of the sales materials needed to perform their job. These items should include:

- Promotional brochures
- Channel lineup cards
- Door hangers and/or Sticky notes
- Personalized Flyers
- Street sheets (turf sheets)
- Hot list
- Sales orders

Logistics

A direct sales representative should plan how you will work territory prior to hitting the streets each day. By using a highlighter a direct sales representative can single out specific homes located on street sheets for visiting purposes.

Depending on how the streets sheets were generated usually determines how a representative will use them. For example, when general turf requests are made the street sheets are usually targeted by selecting the addresses that have "never" been a subscriber. The second choice is subscribers that are "former", meaning they were a subscriber at one point in history.

Finally, a list may be targeted to active customers that are subscribing to only key services a representative may contact to upgrade.

Note: If a direct sales rep needs assistance with driving directions, there are a number of services available for logistics including Streets & Trips®, Google Maps® and GPS applications.

Scheduled Appointments

A direct sales representative must manage their sales appointments effectively. Good organizational skills and time management are vital to guarantee no prospects go unseen. Appointments should be made priority and all other canvassing structured around these time frames.

By keeping appointments organized in a scheduler, cell phone, BlackBerry® or other managed devise, a direct sales representative may track their contacts more efficiently. This practice can help avoid the risk of missing or forgetting an appointment and losing potential sale.

Time scheduling can be very important when working in certain geographic locations. Areas that get darker earlier shorten their time span to work later. By scheduling appointments later in the day, a direct sales representative can spend more time acquiring contacts during daylight hours.

Appointment Management

Daytime	Evening
10am-12pm *Door tagging for afternoon*	
12pm-1pm *Lunch*	5pm-8pm *Scheduled Appointments*
1pm-5pm *Daytime appointments or canvassing.*	

(Example Appointment Management)

Learning the Sales Cycle
Understanding the Sales Process

✓ Introduction/Greeting

✓ Discovery Process

✓ Educating Customers

✓ Closing the Sale

✓ Requesting Referrals

Selling cable services to a customer is a process, rather than an event. Direct sales are made by establishing credibility, relating to a customer and creating comfort zones. These can only be accomplished by engaging with a customer first. This section is designed to provide direct sales representatives effective ways of communicating with prospects and converting them to customers.

Introduction/Greeting

First impressions are significant when trying to engage a new prospect. A direct sales representative only has a couple seconds to gain interest after the initial approach. It's important for a direct sales representative to be neat in appearance and appear friendly and confident. If knocking a door to establish contact, a good practice is to step away from the door and stand approximately ten feet away so the customer has a clear view of the representative when answering. This is especially important when knocking in the evening hours.

By holding up an identification badge, and verbally identifying themselves with their name and company they represent, a prospect is more likely to participate in a conversation with a direct sales representative.

An example introduction could be, *"Good afternoon. My name is Mark with ABC Cable. How are you doing today?"*

By breaking down the introduction a prospect will be pleasantly acknowledged, introduced to the sales person and their company, and posed with a question that requires their interaction. The simple introduction is structured to serve a single action, which is to commence engagement.

Engaging with Touch Points

To engage a prospect a direct sales representative can use touch points. Touch points are moments of interaction between the sales representative and the potential customer. They could include a smile, eye contact, or a pleasant greeting. The more touch points established, the more engagement.

Touch Point Scenario

While at a hardware store, Tiffany was searching for a specific brand of hammer. Her husband had mentioned the brand earlier and she felt would be a good gift for his birthday. Unfortunately she was unable to locate. Immediately an attendant approached her after noticing the frustration on her face and asked if he could help. Tiffany explained to the attendant her interest in the specific hammer. The attendant smiled and offered to look in the back to see if there was any left. After a couple minutes the attendant returned with three hammers of the same brand Tiffany wanted. The attendant explained that the hammers were used for different things. He then asked what her husband uses would be with the hammer. After explaining the attendant offered Tiffany the hammer and asked if there was anything else he could do to help. After Tiffany said no - the attendant wished her a great day.

The attendant didn't make Tiffany feel intrusive to or interrupting him of his job, but rather the purpose it. As marked below the attendant demonstrated multiple touch points including

- *Offered to look in back for brand of hammer*
- *Brought multiple hammers to choose from*

- *Assisted with identifying the best match*
- *Offered additional assistance*
- *Wished Tiffany a great day*

What the attendant accomplished was multiple positive touch points during a single transaction. The attendant could have avoided Tiffany or simply stated they were out of stock without looking. Instead, the attendant was friendly and helpful. Tiffany most likely will share her positive experience with others regarding the transaction. This is called word-of-mouth advertising and it's free.

Shock Value

Creating a shocking statement is a great way to grab a prospects attention. Criteria involved when using a shock statement should be true and relevant to the purpose of the contact. The goal is to relate something about the product or service offering and its benefit to the prospect.

Statements such as "My visit is to make your life a little easier;" "I'm here to save you and your family money;" or "Our internet service is the fastest in town;" are not shocking. Shocking must be thought provoking and descriptive in the benefits provided.

A good example of a shocking statement is "My only goal today is saving you exactly $429.62." What this statement does is peak the curiosity of the prospect as to why

$429.62? Where did the number come from? How can I save that much money? This statement is a teaser and opens the door to the sales representative to now begin the discovery process.

Discovery Process

A direct sales representative should determine the needs and financial ability of a prospect prior to presenting their offer. This means a representative should qualify a prospect and not just take them from introduction to close.

<u>Benefits of the Discovery Process</u>

- Discovery determines wants, needs and desires. Part of a direct sales reps job is to uncover these qualities.
- Discovery provides you with the prospects' financial parameters of what they currently pay for video, voice and data solutions.
- Discovery determines time frame to determine whether prospect wants services today, next week, or a month from now.
- Discovery reveals competition. It allows a direct sales rep to structure their offer with competitors' in mind.
- Discovery helps prevent objections before they emerge. If a sales rep questions and listen attentively, prospects usually tell the rep everything needed to convert them to a customer

Many direct sales representatives try and avoid using the discovery process because they perceive the method to be intrusive. They feel by probing through a prospects needs, current services, financial and purchasing authority, they're in return becoming too personal. Their fear is that the discovery process could risk upsetting the prospect and result in losing a potential sale. The discovery part of the sales process is simply a method used for sharing knowledge.

A direct sales representative knows all about their cable offering including packages and pricing, the prospect knows all about their wants and needs. When both combine the information the prospect can make an educated decision on the services offered. If a sales rep looks at the method this way, they're not being as intrusive as they are trying to provide the prospect with the best solution possible.

Discovery Questions

The discovery process consists of skillfully questioning the prospect to better qualify them. These questions should be focused on what and how they currently use video, voice and data services. Specific information such as channels of preference, features and price can all be found through discovery questions. The answers provided help guide a direct sales rep in the direction of determining the best package.

"What television programs does your family enjoy?"

- This simple question can determine if a prospect is truly loyal to their video provider. If the prospect (and family) predominantly watch channels that are comparable to the cable provider's offering it can provoke education into the channel lineup.

"Do you frequently go to movies or rent movies?"

- This question can pose a cost savings solution if the prospect frequently spends money on movie tickets or rentals. By educating the prospect on premium channels available and Video-on-Demand, the prospect may find viable interest.

"How much do you spend in long-distance each month?"

- This question informs the direct sales representative of how much the prospect is paying in long-distance fees. It can help guide them to the unlimited long distance offer available through the cable provider.

"Might I view a current bill to compare features and rates?"

- Viewing a prospects bill can provide valuable information into their monthly charges, usage, competitive information and more.

For example, a customer can respond with an amount they're charged for their phone service each month. The amount offered may be the promotion fee they subscribed to but doesn't include additional fees. These fees could be line charges, surcharges, long-distance charges, service charges, taxes and more. By viewing the bill a sales representative can point out these hidden fees and build rapport with the prospect.

A direct sales representative may find through these discovery questions that a prospect is paying a considerable amount each month in long-distance charges. This can prompt the direct sales representative to offer a cost savings with the unlimited long distance feature. These simple questions usually fuel additional discovery questions and create interaction between the sales representative and the prospect.

Not all questions should be directed towards saving money. Many customers purchase via perceived value. Establishing value to a prospect can also be performed through the use of discovery questions.

"Are you often waiting for downloads when online?"

- This question can gain insight into any usage problems the prospect has with their current method of internet access. If they possess a slow connection, a direct sales representative can pitch high speed broadband as the solution.

"Have you ever heard of Video-on-Demand?"

- This question can offer a direct sales representative an opportunity to explain the unique service VOD offers. Time is in short supply with many prospects due to work and other activities. By educating them on VOD, a representative can show value of being able to watch thousands of programs around their schedule.

Discovery questions should not be asked in rapid fire mode. This can cause a prospect to withdraw from the interaction. After a question is posed a representative should listen carefully to each response to ensure a mutual understanding. This is called "active listening".

Through active listening, hot button issues, purchase criteria and other valuable information that interests or disinterests the prospect can be learned. Questions can easily be misunderstood, so they should be phrased in a way to have only one clear purpose. Direct sales representatives should also avoid technical language that might confuse a prospect.

Educating Prospects

Savvy customers will research products and services prior to purchase. During this process they will shop around for price, features, functionality and overall value. The direct sales process is primarily an impulse purchasing method to gain customers. This means that the prospect has been approached by a direct sales representative and most likely has not been able to research the product or service prior. To support this statement, direct sales representatives are frequently asked to leave some information behind so the prospect can review before making any decisions.

Often a prospect will call back if the time is taken to review and value is perceived. More times than not, the information and prospect disappear to never to be heard from again. This equates to a missed sales opportunity.

To avoid missing a sales opportunity from lack of research, the direct sales process promotes customer education. Through customer education, a direct sales representative can review the video, voice and data offerings in an interactive setting. A prospect can ask questions and gather feedback and answers from the rep, which is not available when reading a brochure or handout.

Customer education should not be a long and drawn out process, but rather a concise overview of video, voice and data features and benefits. The goal is to inform the prospect of the value in a cable provider's product and service offering.

Example
"ABC Cable Company's High Speed Internet service is 100 times faster than standard dial-up. Imagine what you'll do with all the free time."

"Some key features include always being connected; no need for an additional telephone line; fast access to music and video downloads; online gaming; and compatible with our new digital phone service."

This 20 second educational statement covered:

- Convenience
- Competitive superiority
- Cost savings
- Time savings
- Overall value

In addition, the statement ended with a transitional comment *"compatible with our new digital phone service".* This should help intrigue and prepare the prospect for the next product of education.

Educational Materials

People often request sales materials for reading to process information more effectively. A direct sales representative should provide prospects with informative materials to guide them through the educational process. When discussing video offerings a channel lineup card should be available so the prospect can scan for channels of interest. When data is the topic, a broadband brochure demonstrating speed comparisons between cable high speed internet and dial-up or DSL should be offered. The same should be true when discussing voice. The focus shouldn't be on reading every word within the material, but discussing key features and benefits to express the value.

Once this is shared, the direct sales representative should allow time for the prospect to digest the information, and then answer any questions posed from the presentation.

When answering, a representative should make sure to provide clear and accurate information. If a question is asked that a representative is uncertain of the answer, they should either advise the prospect they will research and contact them with the correct information; or contact a supervisor or manager for direction.

By providing prospects with accurate product and service information a sales representative is educating them on options for their video, voice and data needs. Education is vital in selling because it empowers a potential customer to make an informed decision. If a sales representative can effectively educate their product and service offering, they increase their chances of successfully closing sales.

Closing the Sale

Closing a sale is considered by direct sales people as the most worrisome stage of the selling process. This process is when a representative discovers whether all the sales legwork is going to pay off or whether it's all been a big waste of time. A successful closing comes down to one thing: Knowledge. The more a sales representative knows, the more likely they'll be able to convert a sale.

Closing should occur once the sales representative and prospect have all the information needed to make the right decision.

Getting to know the prospect will help familiarize a sales representative with their needs, providing an arsenal of reasons why the offer is the best match.

When a direct sales representative understands the competition, they can go into the closing with confidence, producing reasons the offer is better for their needs. Although cost is often a factor, it's not always the most important consideration when making a buying decision. Customer service, product quality, and features may also be factors. In some cases, they may even be more important than the cost. A direct sales representative needs to match their strengths with the prospect's priorities, and then be prepared to use that knowledge as leverage in the closing.

Summarizing the Sale

Planning the summary of the sale consists of the knowledge gathered from the discovery (prospect's needs and wants) and services to offer while educating them. To summarize the sale a direct sales representative needs a summary statement. The statement sums up what matched services the representative offers to reach the needs of the prospect.

This is where the direct sales representative uses their problem solving ability to determine the best possible cable package for the customer and presents the package to show value. Summary statements are not interactive, meaning the customer should only listen during this portion of the sale cycle.

"After reviewing your needs for higher speeds I've selected package A for you. This will provide you considerably faster speeds when you surf the web and download files. The package costs only $29.99 per month, but after you eliminate the additional phone line charge and cost of your dial-up account, you will receive faster service for about the same price."

The example summary statement specifically explains the offer, the benefits, and the cost. In addition, the representative explains cost savings through removing the current services which demonstrates value.

Ask for the Sale

Once a direct sales representative issues their sale summary, they need to immediately progress to the next step in the closing process. This step is accomplished by simply asking for the sale.

Too often direct sales representatives make the mistake of asking for the sale with questions like "*Would you like to sing up today?*" or "*Are you interested in any of these packages?*" What happens is the representative has inadvertently handed over the sales control and left it in the hands of the prospect. It's a gamble that costs many direct sales representatives the sale. This happens because sales representatives are not confident with either their offer or themselves. When someone goes to the grocery store a cashier asks them to pay for their products. This is no different.

Closing a sale relies on closing questions. These questions demonstrate a representative's confidence in their offer and perceived value of what is being presented to the prospect. At closing, a representative should never offer an open-ended question, but rather a bold question holding firm because of the value of their offer.

An example of a good closing question would be, *"Would you prefer a morning of afternoon install?"* or *"Will you be paying for your first month with a check or credit card?"*

The only easy answers for the prospect to respond with include either "*morning or afternoon*"; or "*check or credit card*". These questions demonstrate confidence to the prospect that the direct sales representative possesses regarding the value of their products and services offered.

Review Order

Prior to completing the sale a direct sales representative should always review the order with the new customer. During the review specific information should be double checked and confirmed with customer including:

- Installation date & dime
- Sales order completed in full
- Check amount accurate and signed
- Review total costs to customer
- Confirmation of specific services ordered
- Contact numbers home, cell and work
- How many outlets and locations
- Any special instructions

Once the review is completed a direct sales representative should provide the new customer with their contact information. This may be needed if the customer must reschedule their install date or wish to add more services or change packages.

Now that the direct sales representative has completed the sales cycle, they should thank the customer for their time and assure them they'll be satisfied with their purchase. The final step before leaving the customer is gaining a referral.

Requesting Referrals

Successful direct sales representatives appreciate the importance of referrals. A referral is basically a lead and can be more effective than a testimonial. When a sales representative acts on a referral they have been instructed to establish contact. This takes the intrusiveness out of the equation and since the referral was provided by someone the lead knows, it is more powerful than a testimonial from a stranger.

The rule of thumb is to always ask for referrals shortly after closing the sale while the experience is still positive and fresh in the mind of the satisfied customer. It is the belief that if a sales rep can satisfy the customer they can do the same for their friends and family. But why should a sales rep limit themselves to a customer? Why not use the same practice when associating with prospects that haven't purchased or simple contacts in the field?

"Mr. /Mrs. Jones, I know that this may sound strange but the reason I'm so successful in sales is because I generate business through referrals. I do this because I take very good care of my customers. I know that you're not a customer yet, but while deciding on whether or not to give me and my company an opportunity to serve you, could you refer me to someone that may benefit from what I can offer?"

The concept can provide the sales person with a positive uncertainty. This means that even if the sales rep walks out with no sales or no lead, there is potential and hope. Hope can assist in possessing a positive mindset for the next appointment or door knock.

Creating a Positive Attitude

✓ Positive Habit Forming

✓ Handling Rejection

✓ Setting Sales Goals

Possessing confidence is a great trait to maintaining a positive attitude. To establish sales confidence a direct sales representative should constantly realize the value of what they can offer each prospect. Too often a representative worries about achieving sales quota, or contest placement, or other things that become a barrier to the sale. Understanding the benefits of the services offered and how they can improve people lives, is a good start in maintaining a positive mindset..

- Approach each prospect knowing the value of the cable offering.

- Understand the offering may save people time, money and provide convenience.

- Itemize all the benefits the video, voice and data offer provides people.

If a sales rep can feel their offer would be of value to anyone, they have established selling confidence.

Positive Habit Forming

Every direct sales person has faced the disappointment and guilt that comes from setting a goal and giving up on it after a couple of weeks. Sustaining motivation for a long-term goal is hard to achieve.

One solution to this problem is focusing on efforts instead on creating a new habit that will lead to achieving a goal. A direct sales representative can start by focusing not on what they have to achieve over the course of the next month or year, but instead on what they are doing each day. This way a representative is focusing on something achievable. Each day the little change adds up and can make a significant impact over time.

To achieve positive habit forming skills a representative needs to focus on one habit at a time. They should first start by taking their positive habit for a test run for 30-days. Then follow through with the habit each day for 30 days straight. If something prevents the representative from using the habit on any day, they should simply start the process over.

Over time the habit becomes easier and more fluent. Some people only need two or three weeks to effectively form a habit, while others need more time. The key is consistency.

Follow through with positive habits:

- Commit to perform habit daily.
- Set up rewards to motivate.
- Share habit with friends to gain support.
- Track and report your progress.
- Most important - Stay positive.

Handling Rejection

One of the hardest things for a sales person to deal with is rejection. In direct sales a representative will receive numerous refusals, which is why cold calling is challenging. The best thing a sales representative can do is turn a refusal into a valuable experience.

Be objective. Separate the problem from the person. Thank them for their time and for listening. Appreciate their situation.

By reviewing the rejection a representative may learn from what happened. They can think about the conversation, what was said and how it flowed. Think about the body language. Were there any moments when things went awry? What might the representative do different? How might another direct sales representative handle the situation?

The representative should be open and honest. Are there any preferences that they have making them miss things? Is there a pattern of things that are preventing them from selling more often?

The worse thing a direct sales representative can do is take any form of rejection personally. Many representatives feel that the rejected offer is a rejection of them. They can often feel that people don't like them or they have personally failed. The sales industry in general is full of rejections. If it was easy everyone would be selling everything. A direct sales representative must learn to put failures behind them and stay positive and focused on the next opportunity.

Setting Sales Goals

Setting goals are the building blocks to help any door to door sales person succeed. By establishing attainable short-term goals, a direct sales representative can assure frequent victories, building a strong track record and momentum with each one completed.

Performance goals should be viewed as reachable challenges a direct sales representative can obtain. These goals can be chased by reviewing current performance and breaking down what needs to be accomplished to achieve the goal. Some performance goals may include:

- Bonus Tiers on Commission
- Top Team Ranking
- Satellite Dish Win Back Program
- Contest Victories
- Breaking Sales Record

One challenge direct sales people face when trying to reach their goals is where to start. When establishing goals a direct sales representative must make them both reasonable but also worth achieving. Setting an unreachable goal will cause frustration to the point of abandoning the concept. Establishing a goal of no apparent worth may have the same result if the representative feels no sense of accomplishment.

A good exercise is to break goals apart. The first step is selecting a goal and examining it closely. By thinking about the goal one may realize that it is made up of a number of smaller goals, each of which is in turn made up of other smaller goals.

On a piece of paper write down a major goal at the top, and below it, write down the steps to take to achieve this goal. Each of these steps represents a smaller goal, and each of these smaller goals can be broken down further if necessary into more manageable tasks. By reviewing the entire paper a direct sales representative can now see a more obtainable way to reach a goal.

Goal Exercise

List a short-term goal.

_____

_____

Break goal down with smaller goals and tasks.

_____

_____

_____

_____

_____

_____

Break these goals down further with additional goals or tasks to simplify the process.

_____

_____

_____

_____

_____

_____

_____

_____

_____

Once all of the smaller tasks are created, diagnose the amount of time and effort involved in completing. This will provide insight into how to achieve goal.

Chapter Review

This section is to determine the knowledge gained from the previous chapter. If a direct sales rep is unable to provide an answer to any of the questions, they should make note and research to locate the correct information.

Sales Knowledge Quiz

1. List five examples of touch points.

   _____

   _____

   _____

   _____

   _____

2. List three example shock statements.

   _____

   _____

   _____

3. List five example discovery questions.

_____

_____

_____

_____

_____

4. Write a paragraph focused on customer education of digital phone services.

_____

_____

_____

_____

5. List at least three examples of customer education materials.

_____

_____

_____

6. List three example sales summary sentences.

_____

_____

_____

_____

_____

7. Provide three ways of how to correctly ask for the sale.

_____

_____

_____

_____

_____

_____

8. List at least five things to review with customer when finalizing an order.

_____

_____

_____

_____

_____

_____

9. What five things are vital when forming positive habits?

_____

_____

_____

_____

_____

10. List three separate sales goals.

_____

_____

_____

_____

11. Provide a personal goal. Use the breakdown process and provide smaller goals to complete that will help work towards the personal goal.

_____

_____

_____

_____

_____

Sales Knowledge

Use the following section as a guide to create a complete sales cycle process for the example scenarios. Incorporate an introduction/greeting; shocking statement; discovery questions; customer education; summary statement; and closing procedure.

Scenario 1: *Joel recently moved to Detroit from the Boston area and is a lifetime New England Patriots fan. Since Joel now lives in Detroit, his DMA covers the Detroit Lions games vs. New England's. Joe is subscribed to Direct TV® because the service offers "The NFL Sunday Ticket", which enables Joel to watch every Patriots game televised.*

Goal: Leverage the sales flow cycle to sell Joel video, voice and data from cable offering.

_____

_____

_____

_____

_____

_____

_____

_____

_____

_____

_____

_____

_____

_____

_____

_____

_____

_____

_____

_____

_____

_____

_____

_____

Scenario 2: *Freda has been a loyal customer to a traditional phone carrier for over thirty-five years. In that time she has also maintained the same telephone number. Freda doesn't spend much time watching television but does enjoy email and pictures she receives of her six grandchildren, whom all live out of state.*

Goal: Leverage the sales flow cycle to sell Freda video, voice and data from cable offering.

_____

_____

_____

_____

_____

_____

_____

_____

_____

_____

_____

_____

_____

_____

_____

_____

_____

_____

_____

_____

_____

_____

_____

_____

_____

Roll Playing

Role playing is a sales tool used to identify sales strengths and weaknesses. The training tool allows direct sales representatives to simply sharpen their sales skills through using the sales flow cycle.

The goals of roll playing is for the direct sales representative to first memorize and practice their sales knowledge in an interactive setting. Second, maintain control of sales conversation when prospect interaction steers away from the sales cycle. Finally, overcome objections posed in a controlled environment to improve on handling pressure, problem solving, and overall sales conversion.

A direct sales representative should practice roll playing each day with managers, trainers and peers. The following tips for direct sales people to incorporate will help strengthen their selling skills.

1. Make roll playing challenging. Request participants to surprise with random objections and attempt to change subject during conversation. This can help train a direct sales rep on staying on course to the sales cycle.
2. Create a list of the top five objections faced in the field. A Direct sales rep should practice roll playing to overcome these objections and learn how to manage value expectations. This is an excellent method when practiced with direct sales peers

because of the historical experiences and solutions that can be collaborated.

3. Role playing is an educational tool that should be reviewed often. If a sales rep records their sales role playing sessions, they can see first-hand their strengths and weaknesses and work to improve. When seasoned direct sales people fall into slumps, the comparative review of past and present roll playing videos can often assist them in getting back to form.

Glossary of Terms

Analog is a data format that information is transmitted by modulating a continuous transmission signal, such as amplifying a signal's strength or varying its frequency to add or take away data.

ATM (Asynchronous Transfer Mode) is a network technology based on transferring data in cells or packets of a fixed size. The cell size allows ATM equipment to transmit video, audio and computer data over the same network.

Basic or *broadcast basic* is the primary level of service offered for subscription.

Broadband, also known as Broadband Internet, is a type of data transmission in which a single medium can carry several channels at once. Cable TV and B-ISDN networks use broadband transmission, where many local-area networks use baseband communications.

Prior to cable TV, the method of broadcasting cable was called *CATV* or *Community Antenna Television.*

CO (Short for central office) is a telecommunications office that handles the telephone service for that geographic area. Phone lines are connected to the CO on a local loop.

Coax cable is a type of wire that consists of a center wire surrounded by insulation and then a grounded shield of braided wire. The shield minimizes electrical and radio frequency interference.

DBS (direct broadcasting satellite) is a type of satellite used for consumer services such as the transmission of radio and television programs.

Digital Receivers are used to provide digital video formatting from cable provider to subscribers' televisions and often called a "cable box" or "cable converter".

Digital Video Recorder, or *DVR,* acts as a delivery system feeding power from the cable provider to a subscriber's television and allows digital recording of programs.

Disco is commonly referred to as a disconnected customer.

Download to copy data (usually an entire file) from a main source to a peripheral device.

DSL (digital subscriber lines) refers collectively to all types of digital subscriber lines including ADSL and SDSL, which are modulation schemes to pack data onto copper wires.

DSLAM (Digital Subscriber Line Access Multiplexer) is a mechanism at a phone company's CO that links DSL connections to a single high-speed ATM line.

DSR (direct sales representatives), is a term referring to door-to-door sales people.

Footprint is the amount of subscribers and the logistic area your cable plant covers.

Green Bar is the older method of obtaining street sheets named from the paper used in the large scale printers. Green Bar is printouts of current and past customer history used in the cable industry as a guide for direct sales staff when seeking to sell products to new customers or upgrade current customers.

HD, or *HDTV*, is *High Definition Television* that provides service to digital televisions offering twice the screen resolution, higher sound and color than the standard format.

HFC (Hybrid Fiber Coax) is a way of delivering video, voice telephony, data, and other interactive services over coaxial and fiber optic cables. An HFC network works consists of a head end office, distribution center, fiber nodes, and network interface units.

ISP (Internet Service Provider) is a company that provides access to the Internet so a user can browse the World Wide Web and USENET, and send and receive e-mail.

LOS (Line of sight) is a process used when establishing communication between a dish and wireless module to a satellite or wireless tower.

Modem (Short for modulator-demodulator) is a device or program that enables a computer to transmit data over, for example, telephone or cable lines.

MSO, or *Multiple System Operators*, are major cable providers who franchise in multiple locations.

An *Interactive Program Guide*, or *IPG*, is an on-screen guide to cable programming, allowing a viewer to navigate, select, and view content by time, title, channel, genre, etc. by remote control.

Local number portability, or *LNP*, is the ability to transfer an existing fixed-line telephone number assigned by a local exchange carrier (LEC) and reassign it to another carrier.

MDU, or *multi-dwelling unit*, is classified as any multiple family housing units such as a duplex, townhouse or apartment complex.

Nodes are designed to provide service to cable subscribers from the headend. Usually a node is comprised of homes between the amounts of 500 and 1000.

Pay-per-view, or *PPV*, is a pay-tv service where viewers are charged each time they watch a special event or movie being broadcast.

Premium channels represent programming that a consumer must pay additional money to subscribe to such as HBO, Showtime or Cinemax.

PSTN (Public Switched Telephone Network), commonly referred to as POTS (Plain old phone service), refers to the international telephone system based on copper wires carrying analog voice data.

Router (row´ter) (n.) is a device that forwards data packets along networks. A router is connected to at least two networks, commonly two LANs or WANs or a LAN and its ISP's network. Routers are located at gateways, the places where two or more networks connect.

Satellite broadband, commonly referred to as IoS (Internet over Satellite) offers two-way Internet access via satellites that orbit some 22,000 miles above the equator.

SFU, or *single family unit*, is classified as a home or residence occupied by an individual or family.

Sub (Subscribers) is an industry reference for consumer or customer.

Turf is often referred to when describing a sales person's logistic territory to sell.

Upload to transmit data from a computer to a bulletin board service, mainframe, or network.

Video on Demand, or *VOD*, provides viewers a way to watch already aired films and television programs through their digital receivers 24/7.

VoiP (Voice over Internet Protocol), commonly referred to as Internet telephony or VOI (Voice over Internet), enables users by way of Internet as the transmission medium to make telephone calls by sending voice data in packets using IP rather than by traditional circuit transmissions of the PSTN (Public switch telephone network).

Wi-Fi is the name of a popular wireless networking technology that uses radio waves to provide wireless high-speed Internet and network connections.

Wireless Internet is any computer network where there is no physical wired connection between sender and receiver, but rather the network is connected by radio waves and/or microwaves to maintain communications.

Index